Ben Weininger, M.D.
and
Eva L. Menkin

Aging

Is

A Lifelong

Affair

Foreword by Erich Fromm

Preface by Maurice Friedman

Ross-Erikson, Inc., *Publishers*

629 State St., Suite 207 Santa Barbara, California

THIRD PRINTING

Library of Congress Catalog Number: 78-059919

ISBN: 89615-009-7

Designed by Paul O. Proehl

Cover photograph by Rob Jaffe

Contents

Foreword   5

Preface   6

Ben's Introduction   9

Eva's Introduction   12

1. WHO IS OLD?   13
2. BEING DEPENDENT   21
3. LONELINESS   31
4. SPIRITUALITY   39
5. FEAR   51
6. ADULTS AND THEIR PARENTS   57
7. THE OLDER MARRIAGE   63
8. SEX   73
9. ILLNESS   81
10. ANGER AND COMPLAINING   89
11. APPEARANCE   95
12. HABITS AND HEALTH   103
13. ON DEATH AND DYING   115

In Memoriam

Hans Hoffman, Founder, Southern California Counseling Center.
"The intent of the Center was that people have human contact when they need it, and for no other reason than they need it."

and

Rabbi Herschel Lymon, Co-Founder, Southern California Counseling Center, and creator of the programs of humanistic psychololgy of the air, "Come to Life."

Acknowledgments

We would like to thank the following people, who were so generous with their time, read the entire manuscript and made appropriate comments and helpful suggestions: Dr. Thomas Greening, Dr. James Mott, Lawrence Pearson, Janice Chase, Dr. Henry Rabin, Henry B. Burnett Jr., Dr. Edwin Fenton, Neysa Turner, Walter Ganz, Chris Garner, Pat Erlandson, and Olga Naud. Ellen Geiger deserves special thanks for editing our sometimes random thoughts. Thank you to our families for patience and enthusiam: my husband, David Menkin, my children, Judy Hoffman, David Landecker, Anita Landecker, and Peter Landecker; and Ben's children, David, Reuben, Jean, and Rachel Weininger.

Foreword

Dr. Ben Weininger is one of those psychoanalysts — and unfortunately there are not so many — who does not engage in highfalluting theoretical constructions but describes, and if possible explains, the very specific traits of the person he studies, and with whom he empathizes. In other words, he speaks only about what he can see in the other, and not about theoretical considerations from which one builds a construction of the other's personality. This is to say not only that Dr. Weininger is an honest man, but also that he has a penetrating clinical eye, which permits him to see unconscious processes without going into complicated theoretical constructions. It follows that Dr. Weininger can only write about what he has experienced, either himself or in the patient — and one only experiences something in the patient if one succeeds in finding the same trait, perhaps to a smaller degree, in oneself. Such a man can write a book about aging only in the process of aging, but something different holds true for the reader. While this book is very valuable for older people, I believe it is still more valuable for young people. The reason is very simple. To learn how to age must begin in one's youth. If one wants to learn it at a later age, it is probably too late because one has failed to develop in oneself the kind of personality which can experience aging without fear and with equanimity. Although paradoxically this book is one for young people, it would be absurd to say that older people will not be helped by it. It is never too late to see new options and aspects; while it is better to see them earlier than later, there is no point in life at which discoveries cannot be made and be helpful. The book answers many questions without being in the least condescending or sensational. It will help in so far as the written word can help anybody — and we do know that progress in human development has mainly occurred through the power of the written word.

Erich Fromm

Preface

Ben Weininger is a remarkable psychoanalyst, as Erich Fromm has said, and he is something more — a wise man. He has fused Freud, Sullivan, Krishnamurti, Buber, Hasidism, and Zen into a unique distillation of wisdom, courage, grace, and humor that shows itself on every page of this book. For those of us who have been privileged to know him, he stands out as truly unique. As he has grown older his spirit has become ever clearer and more luminous so that he has become for me an embodiment of one of my favorite Hasidic tales: "Get Thee Out of Thy Country."

Rabbi Zusya taught: God said to Abraham: "Get thee out of thy country, and from thy kindred, and from thy father's house, unto the land that I will show thee." God says to man: "First, get you out of country, that means the dimness you have inflicted on yourself. Then out of your birth-place, that means, out of the dimness your mother inflicted on you. After that, out of the house of your father, that means, out of the dimness your father inflicted on you. Only then will you be able to go to the land that I will show you."

This is the land that Ben Weininger has reached and that he helps others reach through this little book, *Aging Is A Lifelong Affair.*

Aging, too, is unique. It is unique, first of all, because it is a dialogue and not a monologue. By this I mean a genuine dialogue, as Martin Buber understood that phrase, not just a literary form. Without Eva Menkin there would have been no *Aging,* and her presence, experience, and understanding come through so clearly on every page that I, who have never met her, feel her presence just as clearly as that of Ben, whom I know well. Genuine dialogue means real otherness — not just two "points of view" or two opinions in a dialectical interchange, but two embodied persons each standing his or her ground and meeting others from that ground.

Aging is unique, secondly, because, unlike most books on this subject, it is not a political, sociological, or even predominantly psychological study, but a multifaceted human treatment of a group of central, interrelated problems that face us all. It is, indeed, as its subtitle says, "a lifelong affair." It is neither just for the old or for the young but for all of us. At the same time, it faces squarely the nagging doubts, fears, and anxieties that plague age, and it reveals them for what they are — problems that can be faced and dealt with, fears of the future displaced on to the present, fears of death displaced on to "growing older," fears of "uselessness" and the loss of social confirmation that goes with it, fears of building that "inner space" that would make it possible for each of us to live fully even in the ever-more restricted circumstances that are, for most of us, the inevitable concomitant of aging. As W.B. Yeats wrote in his great poem, "Sailing to Byzantium":

> An aged man is but a paltry thing.
> A tattered coat upon a stick, unless
> Soul clap its hands and sing, and louder sing
> For every tatter in its mortal dress.

Because aging is a lifelong endeavor, it cannot be restricted to any one sphere. Therefore, this book deals in its separate dialogues, with being dependent, loneliness, spirituality, fear, parents of parents, older marriage, sex, illness, anger and complaining, appearance, habits and health, and death and dying. And it does so in a language and through concrete examples that speak to every person just where he or she is at. I cannot imagine anyone who could not profit greatly from reading this book or who would not find themselves readier for what Ben calls the "venture of life" on completing it.

Maurice Friedman

Ben's Introduction

In this little book, Eva Menkin and I concern ourselves with the phenomenon of psychological aging. We had wondered why many people feel "old" whether they are twenty or eighty, and yet others retain their zest for life at seventy, eighty, or at any age. Over a period of weeks we discussed the attitudes and lifestyles which contribute to the feeling of age. This book is the result of those meetings, and we hope that some readers might start reexamining activities and attitudes in their lives which they have always taken for granted regarding age and aging.

As for myself, I was an only child. I am now 73 years old, though for the past 30 years I have felt rather ageless. I did, however, feel "old" and troubled in my youth, but I was fortunate enough to find individuals and teachers who were able profoundly to affect my view of life.

The deep effect that one person can have on the life of another has been repeatedly impressed on my mind. I had grown disenchanted after practicing psychiatry for only a few years when I met Frieda Fromm-Reichmann, a psychoanalyst working at Chestnut Lodge in Rockville, Maryland. It was Frieda who awakened in me a sense of dedication to both my work and my life. Frieda was the kind of person who usually went a second mile for others — without resentment — and this was her secret.

During the same time I was also introduced to Erich Fromm. From him and his writings I became aware that the patient in my office came there in part because of the society in which we live. My tendency had been to concern myself solely with the patient, his personal history, and his immediate surroundings, including our relationship in the office. I hadn't given much thought to social factors that are often primary in the development of his particular circumstances and problems, and through the years I have often benefited from this reminder. Erich Fromm, Freud, and J. Krishnamurti had the deepest insights into the authoritarian character. From them, I learned about the significance and consequences of the actions of those who blindly follow, without questioning, the authority of another person.

The contributions to interpersonal theory made by Harry Stack Sullivan, Karen Horney, Dexter Bullard, and Lionel Blitzsten have also had a strong impact on the nature of my psychotherapeutic involvement.

As to other influences, I was raised in an Orthodox Jewish community. In my early adult years I discovered the teachings of Leo Tolstoy, Jesus the person, Jiddu Krishnamurti, and later, Martin Buber, all of which helped to awaken me.

From Tolstoy I learned that "Men live by love." When a compass gets shaken up, it moves in all directions, but when it quiets down it always points north. The idea that men live by love was like the North Star. Often I lost my way, but when things got quiet again, there was the pointer, indicating that men live by love.

I learned from studying the life of Jesus that going the second mile did not mean actually going a second mile, but the genuine willingness to do more than is required, without any resentment. I found this an important key, not only to human relations, but to all of life.

At first I tended in my thinking to separate psychology and religion. The work of Krishnamurti has helped me to synthesize the two and see their interrelationship. We need to understand ourselves psychologically, I now believe, in order to arrive at the religious; and to me the religious is Living itself. Psychology helps us understand the barriers and resistance that we set up to living, to moving, to being spontaneous and creative.

Martin Buber is the last of my teachers. Whenever I read his works, I feel a joy in me that I can hardly contain. Remarkably, it is not his person, but the teachings themselves that produce this feeling. As with the traditions of the Old Testament prophets, wonderment lies in the teachings themselves. For Buber, life has meaning only in terms of everyday existence. Buber also rekindled my feeling for my original religion, because I realized through him that denying our earliest religious feelings often diminishes our lives. I feel comfortable seeing our common humanity through the religious feeling of my childhood, although I do not feel compelled to practice the traditional ceremonies of Judaism.

Most importantly, and paradoxically, Buber helped me to be free of all my teachers, including Buber himself.

To the charming and many-talented Eva Landecker Menkin I express my love and warm admiration for sharing this adventure with me and helping make the completion of this book possible.

I would like to express my thanks to Muriel Wood Ponzecchi, Gene Hoffman, George and Bea Wolfe, Micha Taubman, Richard Ogust, and Hallock Hoffman.

> To let go of the past,
> Yet retain a friendly relation to it.
> To let go of one's teachers,
> Yet remain in good relations with them.
> To let go of one's children without regret.
> To let go of one's life and see
> That whatever life we had
> We touched the Eternal.
>
> B.W.

Eva's Introduction

I met Dr. Ben, as he is affectionately called, at the Southern California Counseling Center in Los Angeles in 1972. He and his late friend, Hans Hoffman, founded this unique institution on the premise that good counseling can take place between ordinary people. It was Dr. Ben's theory that almost all human beings have the capacity for caring about others and the abililty to listen to one another in the proper setting. This Center was one of the first institutions in the country to develop and utilize the skills of laypersons, providing low-cost counseling for those who could not afford professional therapy.

I had heard a lot about Dr. Ben and the Center, and when I applied there to be a counselor, I imagined him to be tall, stately, and very wise. I met a small, thin, white-haired man with electric grey eyes and two disproportionally long arms which immediately embraced me in a warm hug. It was the first of many such encounters we had throughout the years, for Dr. Ben is a hugger. He is also a creative thinker and psychiatrist, sharing with patients and friends a vast knowledge of Eastern philosophy and Hasidism, as well as psychological insight.

I don't remember who suggested that we do a series of tapes on aging, but the subject came up often in our conversations. I had written my masters thesis on the psychology of older women, and as my field work had set up group counseling sessions in nursing homes and residences. I later developed programs for older people in such institutions. Dr. Ben was extremely interested in this work and offered to share his experience with me.

Our first recording sessions began in the spring of 1976. We sat in my consulting room and became totally absorbed in our conversation, sometimes missing meals while we examined the many fears, myths, and mysteries of the aging process.

The book which follows was distilled from many hours of discussion. We have purposely used many different pronouns when talking, and we hope that the reader will not be confused by our interchangeable use of them.

None of us escape physical aging, but it is our hope that this small book might help people examine their attitudes towards aging and living. The two are inseparable. This book, therefore, is about living, for people of all ages, as well as for those of us who feel that we are rapidly getting older. If there is joy in life, there is joy in aging.

Our intention here was to impart wisdom rather than knowledge. It is not that we aren't knowledgeable, but as Henry Miller said, "No one has real knowledge. . . only wisdom. . . wisdom to live, but not knowledge about the Universe."

Dr. Ben has the wisdom to live.

Youth had some islands in it, but age is indeed
An island and a peak; age has infirmities,
Not few, but youth is all one fever.

Robinson Jeffers

Who Is Old?

Ben, you've said to me that you've aged with joy. We all hear that aging involves loneliness, pain, fear, ill health, bad temper. So tell me what you mean, what your secret is.

It's not a secret. To be alive is to age, and to me, being alive is joyous. Treating the later years as if they were a diseased appendix to life rather than a vital conclusion is part of the neurosis of our time. I have seen many young people in my practice who feel old, and many elderly people who do not feel any age. Life has no age. If you feel "old," something has gone wrong in life, not with your physical organism, but with your emotions. If we understand ourselves properly and begin to see that life does not have an age tag attached, our lives can begin to be richer, with less stress, anxiety, and fear.

But everyone dreads age. You can't deny that we aren't what we used to be as we get older. We slow down. . . we can't hear so well or see so well. Everything seems difficult. Where is the joy you speak of?

There is no reason for dreading age unless you misunderstand the nature of the living process. No one lives abundantly all of the time, not when young or old. Intense and pleasurable periods in our lives come and go. Aging is not a disease, it's a natural process. A person does not die from aging. When an older person loses his sight or hearing, is nervous or becomes ill, it's because of a physical problem, a sickness. . . not because he is old. If he isn't feeling well, it's not because of aging, but because of other difficulties in life, either physical, emotional, or spiritual.

*It seems as if you are saying that **being** old is natural, but **feeling** old is an indication that a problem exists.*

Yes. We cannot maintain touch with life at all times. Sometimes when we lose touch, we feel old.

I wonder if we need a definition for the word "old"? The way you use it doesn't seem to apply merely to chronological age, but to a psychological disturbance.

To me, feeling "old" is symptomatic of a withdrawal from life. When we withdraw from life, we feel old and tired. I believe that living is eternal and cannot be confined to an age.

You define "old" as a resignation from life. . . but can't that happen when one is chronologically young?

A temporary withdrawal from life can make a young person feel all the symptoms we associate with age. Many middle-aged people also go through periods of "feeling old," but it doesn't stay with them and they eventually become revitalized and alive once more. I doubt very much that by the year 2025 many people will feel old at all. I believe they will feel alive with their particular age. Obviously, they will become chronologically "old". . . have grey hair, wrinkles, and other evidences of aging, but people will not think in those terms.

Why is that?

I feel that young people today are more in touch with their inner life. They care less for the outer images which they might project, and more about relating to the world as unique individuals. When today's young people become older, they will retain the work they did on their inner life when they were young.

That is very hopeful. I agree with you that we have associated age with feeling badly. When a younger person says, "I feel a hundred years old today," they mean simply that they are ill or disturbed or depressed. . . but age gets the blame.

"Old" certainly has a bad name in our society.

And conversely, "young" seems to bring up images of cheer, activity, beauty, and well-being. An old person might say, "I feel young today," when she really means "I feel well and full of pep."

I would not use the word "young" to describe my good feelings. I would say that I feel good about life.

You're saying, rather, that you feel neither young nor old, but good about yourself.

More about life than about myself. We are part of a living organism, and it isn't so much that we need to feel good about ourselves, but about life. If we feel good about life, we automatically feel good about ourselves. . . it's a by-product.

Now I'm beginning to understand your joy in aging, but what is your definition of "feeling good about life?" How does it come about?

We feel good about life when there aren't so many unresolved problems left over from childhood. When an infant is born, and he is held and nursed and has proper loving care, he feels secure and good about life. He can't put it into words. . . It's just part of him. Soon, however, he picks up anxiety from his parents. In our society it is impossible to meet the needs of some infants, so parents act out their own needs and hangups. This is understandable because they picked it up from their parents. The tension and anxiety is transmitted from one generation to the next. Parents misread the needs of their children. The baby might cry because he is colicky, but the mother may think he is hungry. She feeds him, which results in more colic and more crying and produces frustration for both mother and baby. As the child grows older, there are more and more misread needs.

Are you saying that to feel good about life, one needs to have early nurturing. . . that one needs to be cared about in order to feel caring about life?

Yes. If you feel cared about and loved, you forget about being cared about and loved, and just live without concern in that area. When a person experiences losses later in life, they are worked through more easily when one has experienced love and good feelings.

Suppose you haven't been that fortunate in your early years?

Then you need an experience with at least one person who cares about you. It doesn't matter at what age this person appears. If you didn't have a close relationship when younger, and you now have one close person in your life, that makes up for the early deficiency. That person can appear at any time in the life cycle, even on the day of death. One does not need to make up for lost time.

So, at any age, a person needs to feel cared about. Maybe the "joy" in life and aging is the feeling that this is so. Some people never feel cared about, even if they are. Perhaps at eighty, ninety or more, given good health, one can be in touch with life and not feel old.

He who bends to himself a Joy
Doth the winged life destroy;
But he who kisses the Joy as it flies
Lives in Eternity's sunrise.

William Blake

Being Dependent

One of the recurring complaints I hear from older people concerns the pain and humiliation of being dependent on someone. Some people are dependent financially; others need help with transportation, health care, food preparation and companionship. Many feel useless and a burden.

It is a fact that throughout our lives, from time to time we *are* dependent on someone else. Certainly as babies and young children we're totally dependent. Later in adulthood we are often economically dependent until we can make it on our own. For example, I was totally dependent financially on my parents for many years, throughout my training in medical school and as an intern. I feel that being dependent is not a sin. . . it's a human condition which is misunderstood in our puritanical value system. Value is placed on "doing". . . working, being useful. When we are ill or in financial trouble — out of work and needy — we feel useless and dependent because of the value our society places on productivity. Being productive is important, but we don't need to adhere to this value every day of our lives. The older person who feels useless because he is dependent on someone can learn to reorient his values away from work and production. Such people now have time to think and gain new insights, increase their self-understanding and improve their relationships with others. A change of values does seem to be necessary if they are not to feel concerned about being dependent. . . freeing themselves from "doing" to "being." It is the attitude towards dependence which is destructive, not the dependence itself.

This is a good point we especially need to remember when we are ill or otherwise dependent. Another value I find deeply ingrained is "I need to do it myself. . . I must not ask for help." Most older people will not go to a counselor, therapist, or psychiatrist. Many choose to live in isolation and loneliness rather than initiate contact with a person which might lead to intimacy.

This value of "doing it alone" or being independent is just as misunderstood. Some Oriental philosphers say that the healthiest people are totally dependent. One can be dependent in the religious life, as a servant of the Lord. Monks, disciples, nuns, and other religious figures are dependent on everybody for all their material needs. People confuse the word "independence" with self-reliance, and this is a most important distinction.

Really? I never questioned the difference.

Self-reliance means "I can take care of myself but I include you." Independence, on the other hand, means "I don't need you; I am independent of you." Independence is an illusion. We cannot be human and independent. We grow up in families. . . we are born dependent and we die dependent. We can, however, learn to be self-reliant, which is important. Self-reliance means that we can make our own observations and judgments and we may also consult with others. Although the ultimate basis of our decisions has to be our own, we can also value the help and opinions of other people. It is very important to be self-reliant. We need to see with our own eyes. . . hear with our own ears. And we can do this within the context of a dependent relationship.

You said that we cannot be human and independent. What did you mean by that?

Independence leads to isolation and depression. We are social beings. We cannot live totally without other people. Whenever someone cuts himself off from contact with others in the name of independence, loneliness follows, leading to depression, blaming, and irrational behavior.

What about the strong value which independence had in our upbringing? I was rather proud of myself that my children have grown up to be healthy, independent people. In fact, I felt virtuous in promoting their independence. Now you've shattered my illusion.

I believe that what you were really promoting in your children was self-reliance. Somewhere, people have misinterpreted self-reliance and independence. Perhaps this mis-emphasis on independence sprang up when people no longer lived together in extended families, with several generations under one roof. The so-called "nuclear family" feels like a more independent unit. I don't know exactly when independence became such an important and confused word in our lives.

How do you think older people can accept new dependencies they were not able to accept in their younger years? I mean not only physical dependencies, but psychological ones also.

They can accept them if another person is able to reach them emotionally at a deeper level. The older person needs to experience this if he is to develop.

Tell me what you mean by develop.

A child is vulnerable and dependent on his parents, and if he gets hurt, he will close off that vulnerable part of himself. He learns that not being dependent is rewarded, while being dependent is not. That is the developmental process. Now, when that same person becomes dependent because of illness or financial problems, he will remember the hurt he sustained in childhood and insist on being independent rather than risk cultivating a relationship which could lead to a dreaded dependency. He confuses self-reliance and interdependence, which are valuable and essential for life, with independence, which is destructive. For this person not to end up in isolation, it is necessary that some person take a great interest in him and spend time and energy with him. One cannot immediately learn to be open after many years of closing off vulnerable parts of oneself.

I can certainly see that the ideal situation would be to have someone caring who would take that kind of interest in the older person. In so many cases, though, the significant individual in the person's life has died. Sometimes family members are uncaring and preoccupied, or the older person may have experienced an unwanted divorce. She may be living alone somewhere and feeling that no one takes an interest in her anymore. It is very difficult for people to ask for help, to say to someone, "I sure would like to talk to you."

That can be difficult, but I believe that it is always possible to learn. One of my middle-aged patients was getting divorced for the fourth time, and she was feeling pretty depressed and lonely. She went to a restaurant and was sitting alone when an elderly woman approached her and asked if she could sit down. My patient said yes, and they had a very good talk, but when they parted, my patient was reluctant to ask her new friend for her name and address. She would have liked to see her again, but she was not used to taking an initiative, even though the other woman had shown an interest by asking to sit down in the first place. This kind of reticence often prevents us from getting what we need. There is opportunity in everyone's life for making contact, but because of our past training, we often pass these opportunities over. If people followed the Bible's advice, "Ask and it shall be given," they would find more rewarding relationships.

Perhaps it is this great fear we have of being dependent on someone, of "overburdening" people with our problems, which keeps us isolated. And of course, if you risk asking for something, you may end up being rejected. That seems like an awful risk to take for a lot of older people who may have been rejected many times in their lives. Often they have suffered the loss of jobs, self-esteem, health, friends. They consequently feel useless to society. Many older people have told me that they feel of no use to anyone. It's interesting that they say "use." I have a feeling that you don't think of people in terms of being either useful or useless.

Yes, I don't think of people that way. There is a social deficiency in this culture which has created an environment where older people feel "useless," retire early, and die alone in hospitals. In an extended family this does not happen. The old are always a part of the family, and they make a valuable contribution to their culture by passing on their wisdom to the young. This is true in primitive societies. Today, though, older people don't feel wise anymore. We must work to help change our society's attitudes towards the elderly.

And how do you see that we can best do this?

Perhaps by the means you suggested — that we, as older people — become responsible for asking for help and for giving it, that we all become more concerned about one another and work to change our values. It is not enough to be useful to society because we produce. We also need to learn to be kinder to ourselves and others. These are important basic values which are overlooked in our competitive society.

It seems as if young people today have tried to change those values. The stress which their parents and grandparents put on professional achievement, industriousness, and economic security has sometimes been confronted and discarded. Some young people have turned to organic foods, manual labor, and a less competitive lifestyle. They have experimented with communal living and have chosen to de-emphasize money and personal possessions. Older people may see this as loafing, or relaxing moral standards set up by generations of hard-working family members, or an uncaring attitude towards "what is right." I realize that every generation has its "gaps," but this generation seems more apart from its elders than most others.

I think so too. It is a greater leap because the young are still undergoing a kind of revolutionary change. Older people are threatened by this strange behavior, sometimes in dress or living habits as well as working habits, or the lack of them.

Well, if the old reject the young and vice-versa, and if the middle-aged group is busy working to produce and dealing with its own problems, where does that leave the support of the older person?

Old people tend to find it very difficult to accept that they are perceived by society as being old and useless. In so doing, they only make it harder on themselves. The attitudes of the old must be modified. Older people must learn to accept that the things they see around them are true. . . they are indeed seen as old and useless. But they can go from there to build their own support systems. All the aged really need, aside from medical attention and decent housing, are a few friends around, a sanctuary to be a part of. This aids them greatly in dealing with the disapproval of the rest of society. When an older person is in contact with others, he doesn't feel as if he is useless.

. . . And on the faded hangings falls
The chilled uncertain light of
    afternoon: the gloom in which one
Felt so frightened as a child.

Rainer Maria Rilke

Loneliness

So many older people are lonely. Many are widowed after many years of marriage, and in today's society most live alone as long as they can rather than be a "burden" to their children. I know that you seem to have solved the problem by having a sort of extended family; living with your sons, your house-keeper, your ex-wife, and often various clients and friends who are frequent guests at your house. Is this the way you overcome loneliness?

I seldom feel lonely now, but that is not because I live with many people. We are all essentially alone in this universe. We may touch other people temporarily, but never completely. Some people are so frightened of this aloneness that they become very possessive in their relationships. It is one thing to be dependent on others, but it is another thing to be possessive. I am very dependent upon the members of my household and family, but I am rarely possessive. I used to be when I was younger, but I finally found out after many years that I no longer need to possess another person. With that knowledge came a sense of my inner community.

Would you explain this "inner community" and how it developed?

Most of us are afraid of a universal aloneness, of being one small person in a vast and unimaginable universe. We cling to others. . . whether friends, relatives or children. We seek to avoid this terrible aloneness; we feel abandoned when we are left alone by divorce or death or a separation. We have always looked for our support from the outside. When we were young we looked to our parents, later to a lover or spouse, then perhaps, to children. This feeling of being abandoned is actually a carryover from childhood. The small child has no other source of protection and support than his parents. The adult has many other resources. An adult often needs to be alone. If a person can admit that he is indeed alone in the universe, and is not afraid of consciously recognizing this, he becomes part of that universe. This is what I call the "inner community." When you have it, it's difficult to feel lonely. You feel connected with all of life, the life force which some people call God and others perhaps call nature, or many other names. All names refer to a creative force in the universe of which we are a part because we were born. Every person needs to recognize that his center of life, his spiritual center, and his feeling of community is in his aloneness. This is the door through which man must pass, and we keep avoiding that door.

Yes. To face the aloneness for most of us creates a great anxiety. In order to rid ourselves of this anxiety, we join groups, go to church, cling to our family and friends, go out on weekends, work, play. . . do everything not to be alone. Perhaps you are saying that all of those things are our "outside community" and are of importance to us, but they need not be continually available, while the "inner community" is always available if we are only in touch with it.

Yes, I think you have understood, because you have probably experienced that inner community. You feel a part of the universe and of nature.

Well, yes, but I feel I have a long way to go. It's true that I feel a spiritual center in me, but then I have had an outer community for many years and still very much cling to that. I don't know if I actually "cling," in the possessive sense, but I depend on it. I feel I have not really been tested yet. I have loving people all around me.

Even if some of those loving people should disappear, you would find new ones if you have an "inner community." You could then recreate your outside community because you would not be so demanding. You only need a few people in life to be close to.

I have created many new outer communities for myself in my lifetime. I've lived all over the world, each time beginning new associations. I do believe that as we get older this is easier to do. My mother-in-law, who was in her seventies when the family moved to the East Coast, said that it was her easiest move; she had few possessions she wished to take, and she had lost so many people in her life through moving, war, and death that she no longer clung to people as her source of life.

Exactly. Many people believe that older people are very resistant to change. The opposite is often true, for they have dropped a lot of illusions about life. . . life has stripped them of so many. It is easier for the older person to change if the direction is pointed out to him. The reason most people can't change, whether young or old, is because they are going by the old formulas. I am suggesting a new formula, which is to face the aloneness rather than to run from it. This is a new direction, and it means dropping an old formula that says, "I can't be alone, or I'll be lonely."

Is there any other way to get in touch with one's "inner community" except by facing one's aloneness in the world?

There are many ways, and it depends on a person's background and resources as to which ones he chooses. We members of Western culture have a particular problem in finding a spiritual center because of our narrow definition of the word "reality." We call the outside world "reality," and the inner ideas, feelings and fantasies "non-reality." Sometimes we call people crazy who do not share our ideas of reality. In the Oriental philosophies, the emphasis is opposite. There is a pre-occupation with inner feelings and the inner life to the extent that the objective reality of the outside world is ignored. I believe that if spiritual awareness exists, there is no separation between inner and outer reality — there is no feeling of separateness. You belong to your family, your friends, your society, and to the universe. The inner reality is your subjective world and it's just as real as the objective outer world. One of my clients feels that when she is depressed and cannot perform her usual duties, she is not living up to her reality. But she ignores the inner truth, which is that she's feeling depressed. The outer reality she recognizes as "not doing her duty to her work." Her standard of measurement is her performance, while she ignores her feelings. If she could lie around for a few hours when she feels so depressed and just let herself feel badly, rather than jump up, get dressed, and dash to the office, she would probably recover more quickly. She would most likely begin moving around on her own instead of forcing herself to perform. The next morning she's right back feeling depressed, inactive, and discouraged. . . and worried because she can't perform.

What is so threatening to us about this inner world? Could it be that it tries to change our values. . . in this case, our values towards work?

With this client, the threat is to her image of herself. She needs to be an active, productive person all of the time. It is the image which is threatened, not the person. Of course, we hold an image of ourselves because of our values, but all images limit us, because we are fixed and married to that image. We have to maintain it in the face of great inner turmoil instead of living in the "real" world, which is composed of both the inner and outer realities. Any image which we may hold of ourselves, no matter how high, is a handicap — it prevents us from changing.

Are you saying, "Just let yourself be"?

Whatever is, is real. If you're lonely, that's real, so don't fight it if it doesn't fit into your image of outer reality.

Sometimes the outer world can be very cruel and we fight back in our inner world, since it's unacceptable to fight in the outer one. Our inner world holds all kinds of angry and negative feelings which we don't permit the outer world to see. Sometimes we feel terrible about holding on to them, and want to reject them in favor of the more acceptable and familiar outer smile or kind word.

Don't reject any feelings because they don't fit the image and because they don't fit into the outer world. Be aware of them, watch them, just see the way they are. The way we are, is real. If we can understand that those feelings are real, we're less likely to try to get rid of them. They will dissolve by themselves. If you are not afraid of any inner feelings, they will change.

*. . . Tread softly, because you
tread on my dreams*

William Butler Yeats

Spirituality

We've been talking in the previous chapter about loneliness. The loneliest older people seem to be those confined in institutions like old-age homes and convalescent hospitals. You've done some work in this area, haven't you?

Let me tell you about a woman I once worked with in a nursing home. This woman was 83 years old. She'd had a hip operation, and after that, seemed to give up. She forgot names of people; she didn't want to walk or eat. Her family decided they couldn't care for her at home and put her in a nursing home. The diagnosis was senile dementia. Her daughters asked me to see her, and I saw this patient weekly for about a year. We had very good contact and the only sign of the senility was that she couldn't remember my name. We made a joke about that. . . and to remind her I told her it was the first female name on earth — Eve. Although she and I had a warm companionship, with involved conversations about poetry, books, religion, and education (for she had been a teacher), she remained aloof from the rest of the world and often confused with the nurses as to who she was and why she was here. She did not live with the kind of data we call "being attentive to life." That is, she called all the nurses "Ruth," didn't know if it was morning or evening, although she knew the time, and often spoke to people long dead or living far away. In our reading together, we established a close bond, often discussing Emily Dickinson, her favorite poet. During that hour she was completely lucid, wrote and read me her own poetry, and often showed me a journal which she kept daily. The journal revealed her confusion about being in the nursing home and her pain at not feeling of use to anyone. I constantly reminded her that, indeed, she was of great use to me. I liked her immensely and I looked forward to our readings and conversations. Sometimes I would write poetry, which she corrected with great glee. She was still the teacher, and everything she did, she did with great dignity. One day she read me a poem she had written about resurrection. Because it played such an important part in her spiritual life, I'll quote it for you here.

> *I never doubted resurrection*
> *Who yearly planted bulbs*
> *And saw the lilies palely rise*
> *In stiff celestial robes*
>
> *Today I gave again to earth,*
> *This time my other heart*
> *Hold softly, earth,*
> *Remember well*
> *Your ancient mother art*
> > *Nell Worth*

Every time I came for the next few months, she would recite this poem. . . sometimes several times during the hour. Although she read me others, she always came back to this one. It finally occurred to me that through this poem she was trying to tell me something, so one day I asked her what meaning the poem had for her. She hesitated just a moment and then burst into a flood of tears. It was the first time I had seen her cry this way, and we just clung to each other until she could speak. Then she came out with a statement that had been so very difficult for her to make. She said in a very shaky voice, "I really do doubt resurrection." It seemed that all these months she needed to talk about this nagging doubt and had so indicated by the repeating of this poem. With this knowledge out in the open, we could discuss her doubts about resurrection. She had been brought up a Seventh Day Adventist, but had changed to another Christian faith. All her life she had lived with some doubts about resurrection, but had put them aside. Now, it seemed, when she was close to the end, she needed to give vent to them. She then told me that what she really believed is that the only life after death is the legacy you leave behind. Her resurrection, she assured me, would be with her children, her friends, and relatives, in whose lives she would live on. After this outburst, she never mentioned the poem again. It seemed as if she had worked through something very important and seemed far more peaceful. I found an immense release within myself when this woman was able to express her innermost thoughts.

She touched a source of eternal life in herself, and what enabled her to touch it was her relationship with you. She also touched a source of eternal life in you.

Would you elaborate a little about your view of eternal life?

When you finish something, you are resurrected. Life has been going on for billions of years, and presumably will go on for billions more. From the human standpoint, that is the eternal life force. This life force is something which does not die. It always changes into different forms and energy. From our point of view it is forever. . . eternal.

So perhaps this incident connected me with that kind of life force through which my patient and I achieved a spiritual union. It had nothing to do with whether this lady was what the world calls productive, or, for that matter, whether I was being productive, but the energy between us was part of the eternal.

Yes. I'm glad you brought up the question of productivity. As I said before, some of the greatest spiritual leaders did not produce anything. People like Jesus, Buddha, and the prophets did not "work" in the sense which we call production. They didn't even write down their own ideas; their disciples did that. They lived at another level of creativity; they produced inner work. I call it spiritual work: understanding themselves better in their relationships with others, understanding their past and how they came to be, understanding and living their values. Your lady did that kind of spiritual work, and she was able to accomplish it because she had an intimate relationship with you.

You say that great spiritual leaders cultivated their inner lives and this helped them to relate to others. It seems to me that it could also cut one off from others. I have known many people who have taken the so-called spiritual route and have isolated themselves as a result.

That is possible. But if your religion or spiritual life cuts you off from others, it is misunderstood. You know, a priest once went to a wise man in despair, saying, "I have lost my faith." And the wise man turned to him and said quietly, "Well, then, it was the wrong kind of faith." Religion really means community, it doesn't mean isolation. Some people may interpret religion as a hermit-like existence, but all the great spiritual leaders built their religions within a community. The locus of religious feeling may be inside the self, but it is always related to the world, to all of life.

It seems that we keep coming back to that word, "community." Are you talking about an inner or an outer community here?

Both. Three people make a community. Two is a friendship, but three is a community; it isn't a question of large numbers. It's hard to live in this world without knowing two people. When we are younger, especially as teenagers, we need a peer group in order to learn how to get along with people. We need to learn how to get along in a community, and those who don't learn it then, have a difficult time in later life. Fortunately, when we get older we don't really need a peer group, although many have one. We need the communal sense which is our spiritual or religious center, the feeling of being part of all of life and the universe.

So the spiritual quality is that which enables us to be in touch with ourselves, with our environment, with our community, and with life itself.

Yes. We are spiritual from the beginning of life. A child is in touch with life, but loses it along the way. In a sense, we need to recover our child-like nature. . . not a childish nature, you understand, but a child-like nature, involving not only a close relationship to others but also to the world. Martin Buber, in discussing the "I — Thou" concept, tells us that we can intimately relate to a piece of wood we are carving, or a tree we are admiring. We are never isolated if we can relate to life in this way.

Actually, I think that older people and children have a lot in common. One of the things they seem to share is that neither the old person nor the child cares so much about their image. A child is naturally spontaneous, while an older person no longer needs all the impression-building structures that encumber the middle-aged person who is still involved in "making it."

Yes. Older people could be more child-like and freer, and if they could be like that, they wouldn't be depressed, isolated, and lonely.

Becoming more child-like is extremely difficult for people to do, at any age.

I believe that most people direct their attention to what the outside world is doing to them, rather than to what the inner world feels like. For instance, some people become depressed when it is raining; it feels like a hostile intrusion from the outside world. Now if one pays attention to one's reactions to the rain, one can get in touch with one's inner life. We need to pay attention to our reactions, because it is there that we create problems for ourselves. Some people overreact to every situation, feeling hurt and depressed in their encounters with others. We need to pay attention, so that if overreacting is our pattern, we can get in touch with that facet of ourselves and our responses to nature.

Especially as older people. We come to old age with a lot of baggage from the past. It's easy to be critical of the weather, the children, the husband or the wife, the neighbor, or sometimes even God. . . but much more difficult to be in touch with our own reactions and why we react the way we do. It's easier to blame.

We need to look both inward and outward, and always be aware if we are cutting out the sunshine in our lives by how we react to hurts and losses. There's no way of not reacting to those feelings, but we do have some control once we understand our reactions; we have control over whether those hurts go on for days, weeks, or years. We have no control over the feelings themselves because they come on too quickly.

Do we have control over getting over those feelings?

Yes, control over the duration. When I was younger, I used to carry grievances for years, but now I don't harbor them. Actually, I don't work to get rid of them, they drop away themselves. But it has been my life's work to come to terms with my overreactions.

It seems that you have spent at least the second half of your life looking into your inner self, into your own reactions to whatever happens around you. Do most of us get into trouble by letting the outside world react too much upon us?

No. The outside world is always reacting upon us. It's the way we pay attention to it which is important. I can make a mistake and wallow in it, or I can respond differently and learn something from it — but first I must observe my reaction. Then perhaps I can learn from the hurt and not be swallowed up by it.

How does all of this relate to your conception of an eternal life source?

We spoke of turning and looking inward in the second half of life. Today there are many more young people who are looking inward. I feel that when these young people become older, they will continue this inward search. I doubt that they will have the same kind of horror of aging that afflicts many people today. When the inward journey begins early, it remains: you never lose what you have begun.

What have been some of your own spiritual changes?

I was brought up in a totally Orthodox Jewish community. Religion was part of my everyday life. I didn't give it any thought. Then, when I was 21 and a medical student, I had a kind of mystical experience and became interested in other religions and philosophies, beginning with Jesus and later Buddha, Krishnamurti, and Zen philosophy. I've explored these religions for most of my life. It was only recently that I became re-interested in my original Jewish religion, through the teachings of Martin Buber. I grew very interested in the mystical form of Judaism through Buber's interpretation of Hasidism. But it was more than an interest. . . it was the feeling of returning to my own religion, a feeling of being part of a heritage. I think that this is important, because most people who deny their religious beginnings are cutting off a part of themselves. In later life, especially, it is important to get in touch with one's original religion once again, even though one may not believe in all of the dogma and doctrines. I am convinced that to deny feeling a part of that religion, whatever it is, is a repression of an important part of oneself.

Do you feel that this can be done by an older person?

Yes, we need to realize that we must look first to our own background in order to have a life with wholeness and meaning, even though we may have rebelled against it at one time. We must feel a part of our traditions, be they Christian, Jewish, or any other.

Wouldn't that perhaps also get us in touch with a religious community as a possible source of support?

Yes. We would have a greater feeling of community even if not actively involved.

The theme of community keeps coming up, again and again. As I understand it, even an internalized community of a faith that was once taught us keeps us from living an isolated existence. You talked about your mystical experience as a young medical student, and it seems that now in your later years, you are again attracted by Hasidic mysticism. I'm curious as to how that mysticism attracts you and how it differs from a religious experience.

A mystical experience is difficult to explain; it needs to be experienced. It gives one a sense of feeling whole, a sense of belonging to the world, the universe, and to the community. When I first had this experience, it gave me such a feeling of ecstasy and joy that it seemed to erase every other experience.

It sounds like "falling in love."

Yes. Before this experience happened, I was in a state of distress and anxiety, often a state when one is ready to fall in love. . . only this was a love of God. I put a lot of stress on the mystical thing, trying to get the feeling back when it left me. This is where I made a mistake. I thought it of great importance to hang on to the feeling. . . many people interested in the mystical life make that same mistake. But now, from my new understanding of Hasidism, I see that it is important not to make the mystical experience or the "satori" experience or the "nirvana" experience an end to itself. The awareness of that wholeness needs to be applied and experimented with and lived in everyday life. Unless we can bring that which we have learned into day-to-day life, we miss the point of the communal. We are social animals and we need to rediscover the social quality in ourselves.

Fearlessness is the first requisite
of the spiritual life.

Mahatma Gandhi

Fear

Fear is a feeling we deal with all of our lives. But as we get older, fears seem to mount up. . . we start to fear aging itself, being left alone, not being able to cope anymore, not having enough money to make it until the end. And, of course, there is also the universal fear of death. How can an older person overcome some of those fears? They seem so justified.

Fear of being alone, like the other fears, has two aspects to it: first of all, yes, there is an objective real possibility of being left alone, not having any more friends, losing a spouse, having children move to distant places. Secondly, there are inner fears that have not been resolved in early life: fears of abandonment in childhood which have carried over into adulthood and now into old age. This psychological fear is not rooted in reality but in a basic mistrust of life. We have to look at it from that standpoint. We cannot do anything about the guarantees which we believe the world offers us.

What about the fear of death? That too is a basic mistrust of the life process, a lack of faith.

It's the same thing. We cannot do anything about the reality of being alone or about death, but it is not a fear of physical death or of being alone, but rather a fear of change. It is the great fear of the unknown. It is a fear of letting go of the familiar. How we cope with this fear depends largely on how we have coped with previous changes in our lives.

Perhaps there is also a fear of being empty inside, of not having the inner resources to cope with the world anymore.

Yes. Usually life itself fills up emptiness; just getting up in the morning, washing, having breakfast, writing a letter; the ordinary things occupy the empty spaces. If a person has been hurt a lot and has built barriers around himself, however, he will be reluctant to expose himself to others for fear of being hurt again. If this happens, a large part of that person remains hidden and unavailable even to himself. This means the person is not living fully and probably never has. Such a person would find it more difficult to be left alone than, let's say, a person who has been able in the past to live fully for most of the time.

By "living fully" do you mean keeping active, busy, involved?

Not necessarily, but certainly involved with life. In order to be involved with life you need not be doing things continually. The great thinkers of the world have been pretty passive and have been dependent upon others to do their "business" for them. As I said before, being involved with life is an inner process which connects one to the universe and all that is in it. It also means an involvement with at least one other person.

Does this mean if a person has been hurt so much that he has shut down a large part of himself, he will be doomed to fears of isolation and change? Is there anything that he or she can do?

The way a person lives now determines what happens to his feelings later. . . not necessarily what happens to the person, but what happens to his feelings. So, if such persons are afraid of being left alone now, they need to look at what is blocking them now. If they were living fully now, fear for the future would disappear.

I'm hearing you say that fear is really for the future rather than the present. Is that correct?

It is almost impossible to be afraid in the moment. Fear usually involves a concern about the future. Fear of the future implies an unpleasantness from the past projected onto the future. Since you never know the future, you anticipate it from past experience. If I am afraid that a dog will attack me, my fear is for the next minute. I am not yet attacked, I am not yet hurt. The fear comes from my past experiences with dogs who look like this, perhaps what others have told me about dogs, or things I've read. While I'm paralyzed with this fear, I'm really still O.K. at this moment.

Of course you're right. At the actual point of danger, when we are really involved with the crisis, we are no longer afraid. We're much too busy acting. If the dog had attacked you, you'd be fighting him or yelling for help.

If we had a problem with fear, we need to look into what is blocking us from living more fully in the present. It is not necessary to live to the optimum, but more fully. We need to reevaluate our expectations from life and see if they were valid in the first place. Was it reasonable to assume that we would never be alone, in despair, without money? Who promised us such a paradise? It is never too late to reevaluate, and change our expectations of life's "guarantees."

Well, it seems as if one of life's guarantees in contemporary society ought to include some kind of economic security for older people. At least this would be one of my expectations. I mean, I would like to be able to live out my life in comfort, having done my share of the work in my society. I really don't want to change that expectation.

Well, this, like other fears we have discussed, is a compound problem; some of it is valid and some is a lack of faith. I too have the fear of economic insecurity. I feel that I'm not going to get to the end with the money I have. This means that I have a basic lack of trust in this regard, and I need to work on that. Although there is a validity to my economic plight, there's also an irrational fear. There is room for new understanding in this area, and I am working on it.

You have children and influential people in your life who, I'm sure, would see to it that you have a comfortable old age. But I do see your irrational fear. I've heard people say, "My children lead their own lives and have their own families, and I don't want to be a burden. . ." But what they are really afraid of is that no one will care for them and they will end up in some obscure nursing home where they will vegetate and die alone. That kind of thinking does represent a lack of trust, but it seems to me that it also indicates a feeling that they are unloved, which may or may not be true. It probably is true if they maintain that position long enough.

In my case, I feel that my children will be able to take care of me, and I don't think that this would interfere with their lives. I always gave them the first priority over everything else, and they would gladly share what they have with me. So really, my inner fear about not having enough is not based on what I know to be true. I look at my fear of economic insecurity as a lack of faith and a lack of touch with my full life resources. Gandhi said, "Fearlessness is the first requisite of a spiritual life." We can do very little about the reality of poverty, of being left alone, or the fact that we must die. We can only pay attention to our responses to these realities and deal with them accordingly.

You honor your parents most by growing up yourself.

Dr. Ben

Adults and Their Parents

One of the most important relationships an older person has is with his family, especially with children and grandchildren. Yet, these relationships are often strained, misunderstood, and, in extreme cases, severed. How can older parents and their middle-aged children understand one another better?

We have to consider this problem from two stand-points, from the view of the older parent and from the position of the children. First, let's talk to the middle-aged child about his parent. If he is serious about getting along better with his parents, he needs to change his ideas about what it means to be an older parent, and what the needs of that parent are.

Can you elaborate on this?

Very often, an older child feels burdened because he thinks the parent demands too much of his time. He also feels guilty about not giving enough, living too intently in his own world with his own family, and generally feeling inadequate and helpless in the relationship. Actually, most older parents don't need nearly as much time as the child thinks. One of my friends visited her older parents recently for ten days. After the sixth day, she began to feel very uncomfortable. However, she stayed the entire ten days and a visit which began satisfactorily became irritating and strained. If she had stayed only six days, her parents would have appreciated those few much more than the full time planned, which turned into a hostile situation.

Your friend's idea then, was that she was going to have ten days to spend with her parents and she decided to grit her teeth and get through them, rather than leave while the relationship was still good.

Yes. This is what is unclear to many people: that it is not a question of length of time spent, but rather the quality of the time involved. It is the quality of the relationship which is important. . . being fully there for the parents for a short period of time.

Is this what you mean by changing one's ideas about what older parents need?

Yes. Actually, I believe it is true for everyone. If we could have someone's full attention for short periods, we wouldn't crave constant attention. To get back to the middle-aged children, I feel that they would be less anxious if they thought there would not be such a great demand on their time. It's a misconception on their part that there is indeed such a demand. You see, it becomes a vicious circle. If I am afraid that there will be a great demand on my time, I become anxious and want to run away. This makes the older person anxious about my wanting to leave, so the older parent becomes more demanding, and the more demanding he becomes, the more I want to leave.

So you have two anxious people in a vicious circle.

And in order to break the circle, the younger person has to see that his perception of the older person's needs are mistaken, that if he were fully there and attentive, the demands would decrease.

How about the parent who has never stopped being critical? You know, the one who's constantly saying, "Why don't you get a better job?"; or "You really should get a new couch"; or "Why don't you change Junior's piano teacher?"; "Your hair needs cutting, dear."

This is another point which younger people don't see about their older parents: that often they give instructions and tell them what to do because they genuinely want to be good parents.

But who needs a good parent at age fifty or sixty? We've all had our fill of parenting by then and would rather sip tea with them and try to be friends.

Ah yes, but that is only possible if the children don't over-react to their parents' instructions. Actually, parents are anxious if they don't feel too welcome and revert back to parenting, with which they are familiar. But their instructions need not be carried out. If you understand the reason behind the message, it is possible to ignore the instruction and change the conversation.

Well, I can see whose side you're on in this battle. Now, tell me how the older person can contribute to improving the relationship. We've talked about the middle-aged child becoming more supportive, more patient, and more attentive; but what are the responsibilities of the older parent?

I will talk now to the older parent and say: If there is a problem with your children, it probably means you want more of them than they can give you. One reason you want more than they can give you is that you don't have enough other interests in life. You have made your children and grandchildren the entire focus.

That can begin very early in parenthood and last a lifetime. I know very many young parents, especially mothers, who feel virtuous because they have devoted themselves exclusively to their children. All outside interests focus on them alone, so that even if the mother has other activities, they are child-related groups such as P.T.A. and Cub Scouts, which are dropped when the children grow up. Unless she gets herself some new interests, that mother is in trouble.

Yes. In that case she will probably cling to her children as her main source of life.

How can she develop new interests in later life when she has spent a lifetime focused exclusively on her children? How can she stop her clinging?

First, she needs to be aware of her "clinging." Just the awareness itself will free her a little; just seeing it will change it slightly. The older woman, however, does not see herself as clinging; she only sees that she'd like to have more of her children, and they are not available. So if she sees how she contributes to the situation, she will be freer to pursue some other interests. Now, these interests need not be new. Often earlier interests can be reactivated. I myself returned to a boyhood interest in chess lately. The important thing is to develop a community of your own which does not involve the children. It doesn't exclude them, but it doesn't necessarily include them either.

We keep only that which we set free.

Unknown

The Older Marriage

It used to be a tremendous shock when an older marriage broke up. After thirty or fourty years, it was assumed that a marriage had stabilized. Yet today, the older marriage is in trouble. Now that the couple is in their fifties, sixties, or seventies, the children are gone and their lifestyle has changed through retirement, how can they view each other as a support system?

Many of these marriages fall apart because the couple doesn't have much in common. They had children too early, before they really had a chance to know one another well. They didn't have an opportunity to become friends, only lovers. After the passion of love subsided, they looked for substitutes, perhaps in a job or other people. Now, when they are older, they try too hard to have some kind of relationship, but they don't know on what basis. In my opinion, the basis needs to be friendship; once the couple can become friends, sex and companionship will become part of the relationship.

How does one learn to be friends, after one has just "been around" for the last twenty-five or thirty years? Or what if the couple has grown in different directions?

They could see if they can discover some common interest, even if some of their interests are diverse. He might like golf, and she might like tennis. If they both like to garden, that could be a beginning of a friendship. I'm thinking of one common interest in particular which could initiate a friendship, that is, understanding yourself psychologically. Basically, that is a common interest for most people; we all have a self that needs to be understood.

You make an interesting point. Most books, articles, and wise people tell us we must understand our partners, our children, our friends, our enemies. But you say, we must understand ourselves in order to be friends, and we must be friends in order to maintain a marriage.

Yes. We all must work to understand ourselves better. In that process, we might find that we have a common spiritual center, we would have to include others in our environment.

What is a common spiritual center, and how can two people acquire it?

A common center can be reached when the partners explore and perceive their own behavior. The way we usually react to our partner or to other people is not spontaneous. The feelings we transmit come from the way we reacted to parents when we were children. Our parents had certain requirements and expectations of us which may not have been suited to our talents and needs. Being children and dependent, we had to learn to cope with our parents by being either very submissive and resentful, or by being rebellious in order to maintain some kind of integrity.

Are you saying that we carry these resentments into our new intimate relationships?

I am. Whenever we are intimately involved with another person, these old patterns of relating surface. We feel hurt, angry, humiliated, submissive, and resentful, rebellious or aggressive. The old patterns which we used as tools for survival with our parents have been brought with us into adulthood. Usually they don't work with our new intimate partner, and therefore we feel misunderstood and unloved, the way we felt as children, and we withdraw into our former neutral state. This sooner or later becomes boring and lonely, so we seek a new relationship and begin the pattern all over again.

Can that pattern ever be broken?

Only when we understand and see, really perceive our behavior in the world, not only with our partner, but with others. This mature self-exploration and understanding can then lead to a common spiritual center.

The spiritual center, then, is a new understanding, a new way of behaving and "being in the world"?

The spiritual center is the "NOW". . . the present, not the past. The behavior patterns from the past belong to our history, but we need new behavior to cope with present situations. If we understand ourselves in our relationships, we can react in the present authentically and spontaneously, and not from inadequate responses from the past. If both partners are in the here-and-now and understand how they relate, they have a common spiritual center.

Let's see if I can put that into an example. Suppose my husband is very bossy. He has always had authority, and he needs this in order to feel good and "whole." He wants me to come "right now" and help him place some new plants around the garden. My own reaction is to resist that kind of demand, but I understand that resistance in me. It is a resistance to commands and authority. Since I understand it, I don't need to act out of the past, which would have meant pouting, feeling hurt, and angry and resentful. Instead, I can authentically say that I'll come as soon as I can, and then we can share a good experience planting, since we both basically really enjoy it.

You were feeling good about yourself as soon as you became aware of your resistance. It's true that if one partner learns self-understanding, they can often take the other partner along until he or she sees the importance of the inner self.

Well, I hate to tell you, but my experience in counseling older married couples or ex-couples has been the opposite. Typically, one partner has had counseling and has some self-understanding, and the other partner has steadfastly refused help. Often the result is a split after many years of marriage. Do you see that split as healthy, or do you feel that the partners will make the same mistakes in new relationships?

More people live longer now than ever before. It used to be that after the children were grown, the couple had completed their task. They might live together another 10 years or so, but usually one or the other died after that. Today the couple might have another 30 or 40 years together after the task of child rearing is completed. There now is a question in their mind as to how they could spend those years differently, more productively. Sometimes they decide to spend those years with a new partner, or without a partner.

That seems to be happening more and more, that people change partners in later years.

Living longer may itself become a threat to the marriage. It seems to me that one intimate adult relationship for so many years may not be enough. That does not mean that one marriage is not enough. It simply means that one needs more intimate friendships. Some people have been so traumatized in childhood that they might need half a dozen intimate relationships in order to work through their unresolved problems with them.

Can you elaborate a little on that, please? How do you see us resolving early childhood problems in intimate relationships?

When you become intimately involved with another person, your past unresolved problems come out: possessiveness, jealousy, competition, doubts about worthiness. These problems appear in every new relationship. If the problem is very intense, like the fear of rejection, it may be very difficult to work it out in just one intimate relationship.

So you feel that it can be worked through in many different relationships?

It may be worked out with more than one intimate relationship. Sometimes the therapist functions as another intimate person with whom these conflicts may be worked through. Sometimes, however, if the trauma is too great, the person may need more than a therapist and more than one relationship; sometimes someone needs to repeat again and again the conflicts which remain unresolved. That is one of the functions of intimate relationships.

When you talk about intimate relationships, do you mean sexual relationships as well as loving relationships?

It isn't just sex and love, though certainly they may be a part of the intimate relationship. It's learning to love — you learn to love to the degree to which you have worked out your past problems.

So, if you've had the opportunity to work through these conflicts with many different people, then, say at 70 or 80 or so, you should really be in good shape.

Right. You might find that you can then live with one person for the rest of your life. Or, perhaps you don't need an intimate relationship with one person at all. You can have many friends without even needing an intimate relationship. It's not absolutely essential to a person's life, but it is a longing, especially with people who feel that they have not been adequately loved.

I still wonder, if the old marriage fails, and there is a new relationship or marriage, do you see that as just another opportunity to work through more conflicts? Or do you feel that perhaps at last a person can settle into an intimate relationship that is not tainted by those early problems?

It's possible. They would both have to have a certain degree of interest in themselves and be willing to work on their own problems independently of the other partner, yet in relationship to the other partner and to those around them. If we still retreat when we feel threatened, withdraw, fight, and blame, we do not yet understand ourselves. But if we let go of the old reactions, instead of hanging on to those patterns of behavior, we have a good chance of living a full life together with one intimate person until the end.

Well, you've given me some hope.

I predict that marriage will eventually become an individualized contract.

Do you feel that in this way the relationship would last longer and be more fulfilling?

I think that with individualized contracts, the relationship will last longer. If you believe you will be married for life, you might begin to abuse your partner, but if you know that the marriage will terminate if it becomes destructive to you and the children, you will be more considerate of one another. You will always have the choice to leave.

The paradox in what you're saying seems to be that if we don't expect a partner for life, and instead make a contract periodically, a contract which runs out periodically and has to be renewed, then perhaps we will stay married for life because we have an alternative and we won't feel so trapped.

Yes, but not only would the trapped feeling be minimized, but also the feeling that one can abuse one's partner with impunity.

Love at the lips was touch
As sweet as I could bear;
And once that seemed too much;
I lived on air.

Robert Frost

Sex

The subject of sex is no longer the mystery it used to be, but there exists a persistent belief that sex is not for the old. Old people have come to believe this themselves and often feel that their sexual lives are over, or that they are sexless after 50, 60, or whatever magical number they care to name. Birthday cards tend to prolong this myth by endless jokes about the loss of sexuality as one gets older. How do you see this problem, or do you see it as a problem?

One of the difficulties is that people associate sex mainly with intercourse. This is one problem. In Freudian language, we use the word libido, which is a kind of sexual energy that need not necessarily be expressed in intercourse. Actually, friendships, close friendships, have an erotic coloring to them. We are all erotic, libidinal people all our lives if we have any affection for anybody. So if we could disassociate intercourse from being erotic in a close friendship, it would cease to be a problem.

Are you saying that intercourse is not an important element in the sexual life of older people?

People are capable of having intercourse throughout their lives. A man is physically able to have erections (although not as many as when he was young) at any age, unless he is ill. A woman may experience less secretions, but this can be taken care of by hormones or lubricants. There is no physical reason why two people who have a close relationship can't have intercourse from time to time all of their lives. I am saying that intercourse is not the problem. . . closeness is. If there is closeness between two people, it implies sexuality. Intercourse may or may not be a part of that close union.

It seems as if you make a very weak case for sexual intercourse when society puts so much emphasis on this aspect of sexuality.

The whole problem of sex becomes a burden when you are preoccupied with it. It's really simple. If you have a loving partner and you want to make love, you make love. If it becomes a preoccupation, it turns into a problem. You either do it, or you don't do it. It really doesn't affect your health or happiness, but worrying about it does.

Then perhaps it becomes a preoccupation if we feel that we need to be competitive in sex, as we are in other areas of life, and do it better, more frequently, and with grander techniques than anyone else. Sexual activity in this society seems to be some kind of index to how manly or womanly a person is.

What the real problem is in sex with young or old, is a fear of being close to others. If a person is afraid to be close to another, he shuts off the sexual part of himself. If he is open to other people, he needn't concern himself with whether he has sexual intercourse or not. Being sexual is touching someone's hand, hugging, and kissing, as well as having intercourse if that is desired.

So you're saying that as long as two people have a good relationship, they will naturally be sexual, libidinal people, affectionate towards one another in friendship or love, and can choose to have intercourse or not without guilt or hostility.

You mention guilt and hostility. When hostility begins in a relationship, sexual interest declines. This is the first thing to disappear when hostility enters. It is interesting that this carries over to the animal kingdom. If an animal is threatened, the first thing it loses is sexual interest.

So if potency declines, and there is a loss of sexual interest, it is usually due to a break in the relationship or perhaps boredom or actual hostility.

Yes, but we musn't lose sight of some physical reasons which may appear with age. I'm reminded of the famous analyst, Theodore Reik, who wrote about having intercourse with his wife in later years and became panicked when she turned blue. The physical factor may certainly play a role in the capacity to enjoy intercourse, and a doctor may have to be consulted if a heart condition is present. Otherwise, if a person is reasonably healthy and has a responsive partner, there is no reason why an older person can't have as full a sex life as he wishes. I repeat, however, that I have seen many people who have a close, affectionate relationship without intercourse, and this does not mean that they are non-sexual.

I'd like to dwell for a moment on another aspect of sexuality. The fact is, that after the age of 70, unfortunately, there are about three times as many women as men. These women often do feel asexual, although they long for affection from and for a man. As you describe libidinal energy and sexual intimacy, is it necessary for women to have a male partner, or can women be intimate in close, caring relationships which in your terms are sexual?

Yes, two women can have a real and affectionate relationship; they can be very close and open, which would be just as fulfilling as if they were with a man. We are fixed and frozen into the position that the partner must be a man, but it need not be. Again, this kind of relationship need not be sexual in the genital sense if the partners do not wish it. Orgasm, whether from intercourse or masturbation, is a way of relieving tension; it is not necessarily a way of having an affectionate relationship with another person. Frequently, intercourse is not about love at all, but about relieving tensions.

So perhaps, if the older person keeps intimate relation-ships with the other sex or the same sex, he can express his sexuality all of his life through affection and love.

Yes. I believe in many hugs a day. It's regenerating. I don't find that at my age making love is essential, although if I have a responsive partner, I still enjoy it. What is essential to me is affection and hugs. It's like food. I don't need nuts in my diet, although from time to time I like them, but I do need fruits and vegetables in order to feel good.

You're saying that it is part of your human need to give and get affection and to be close.

Yes, but not all the time. It's not possible to be close all the time. People need some distance from one another, too. In a trusting, open relationship, this request for distance is recog-nized and granted.

I brought up the problem of the older woman. Now, what about the older man? Suppose he is an open, affectionate person, like yourself, and he loves to hug and be close to women, all women. Our society labels him a "dirty old man"... and is repelled by the idea of his sexuality.

Here again, I think the confusion arises because we associate only intercourse with sex, not affection or openness. Society believes that a man wants intercourse when he really wants affection. It should also be permissable for older women to have young male friends, and older men to have young female friends in an emotional, affectionate, erotic way. This might sometimes lead to intercourse and sometimes not. Unfortunately, the association in people's mind is that all sex leads to intercourse.

I've had older clients tell me, "Oh, I wish I could find a husband again. I would love to have the companionship. . . I need to give to someone and be cared about, but I don't really want sex anymore. I've been through all that."

I would say that these women close off a large part of themselves, their open, emotional, giving, and receiving part. Otherwise they wouldn't even think about the sexual aspect. . . that's a by-product of closeness; it just happens. But if she's concerned and says "I don't want sex," she has a problem, not in the sexual area, but in the "being close" area. . . the giving and taking area. She wants companionship and friendship, but if she were really open to it, she would allow her sexuality to evolve.

I was wondering, we've been talking about sexuality in the older person. How much of what we have said applies to the young and middle-aged person as well?

Anything I said about sex applies to everyone, young and old. Sometimes a younger person is overanxious about performance because he doesn't know how to deal with intimacy. Since he or she fears closeness, he puts emphasis on the technique and prowess of intercourse. Intercourse can be a way of avoiding intimacy. It's easier sometimes to have intercourse than to be open and vulnerable to another person. The older person usually does not put such emphasis on performance, having learned a more quiet and gentle way of lovemaking. When one is quiet, one can be more aware of the other person.

I think that older people, if they are in touch with themselves and their own sexuality, can really teach the rest of society something about love and affection in sex. It seems to me that the young have all kinds of fantasies about what goes on in the bedrooms of the aged. These erroneous images interfere with seeing the older person as a whole human being with needs to love and be loved.

In this short Life
That only lasts an hour
How much — how little — is
Within our power!

Emily Dickinson

Illness

So far, we have been talking about the well person. We've discussed adjustment to the various fears associated with aging. It's one thing to make adjustments and changes when you are in fairly good health, but what about the chronically ill person? What about the pain of arthritis, heart disease, stroke, and problems with hearing and seeing?

When we are young and get sick, although we really feel sick and miserable, the illness is temporary and we know it will go away. As we get older, we're more likely to have chronic diseases. We may not necessarily feel so sick with them, but impairment usually occurs. The question then becomes "How do we deal with impairment?"

I see what you are saying, that there is a difference between the acute illness which we know will pass and a chronic illness which we need to learn to live with.

An impairment means a restriction on your activities. It does not mean a restriction on your life. There is a very big difference here. I have lived with restrictions for some sixty years. When I was 12 years old, my parents were told I had a heart disease. They thought I wouldn't live very long, and they took great precautions. I was restricted in my physical activities, but it hasn't interfered with my life at all. I merely had to restrict myself in that area.

Maybe that kind of physical limitation pushed you into intellectual activity and helped you in your spiritual pursuits. Your impairment isn't noticeable; you move like a young man, and your energy seems boundless.

Let's take someone like President Roosevelt; you could certainly notice his affliction. Although he was paralyzed from the waist down, this limitation didn't ruin his life. We have to be most clear on the fact that his restrictions were all in the physical area; he couldn't even stand up to make a speech towards the end. Paralysis is a very real restriction on someone who loves physical activity, but life is more than just moving about. Some of the great writers, artists, and even sports figures have had illnesses which resticted them greatly, but they lived their lives fully and accomplished great things.

So again, perhaps we blame age on infirmities which can strike us down at any time of life. Age doesn't seem to have to be a factor in our fears of illness. Often we are more able to cope when we are older. . . having had a lot of experience with reversals in life. It's a fact that if we live long enough, we certainly will have to cope with restrictions. The way you describe them, they don't seem as horrifying as our imagination leads us to believe.

That's true. For instance, at the Southern California Counseling Center in Los Angeles, some of the finest and most sensitive counselors are handicapped people. One woman does counseling from a wheelchair. She has multiple sclerosis and can move very little of her body, and she speaks with difficulty. She not only counsels, but teaches other counselors and supervises their work. There is also a blind counselor, whose dog accompanies her into the rooms with her clients. The oldest counselor is 85, and her clients greatly benefit from her wisdom and understanding. All of these people are involved with life and their chronic conditions, although greatly restrictive, do not interfere with their inner involvement with themselves and their commitments to others.

I think that what is threatening in these disabilities is our image of ourselves as whole people, both physically and psychologically. We want so much to be perfect specimens. Not only that, but there seems to be pride involved, the pride of being able to take care of ourselves.

Yes, but it's a false pride. You're right in noting that we have a great stake in maintaining an image of ourselves. This image restricts us just as much as a disease or handicap.

Then perhaps a mobilization of that inner community is needed to change the image from a vital, healthy person to a restricted one when we become disabled.

Basically, you shouldn't see yourself as restricted if you live reasonably fully. Life has no boundaries. When you are living, it feels as if you contain the whole universe. Living can't be put into a box. . . you can't confine it. If you "change" one image for another, you still maintain an image. The image might now be, "I am restricted." But there is no basis for having such an image. Young people need an image, a good image of themselves in order to feel loved and productive. An older person, however, has had so much experience in life that he doesn't need to hang on to those earlier images. They only get in the way, both images of ourselves and images of others.

I guess you're saying that all images of ourselves are unnecessary to keep us from living in the present. Probably most images are false, anyway.

That's true. Actually, when you are restricted physically, it becomes necessary to shift attention from outer activities to an awareness of your inner nature. If your interest is still focused on the outer world and you need to lie in bed, it will be a very distressing time for you. You lie there bemoaning the things you used to do. If the interest shifts to an inner exploration of self, however, you develop a new way of looking at life. Then the restriction does not feel like a restriction.

And does one need help in doing that?

Yes, you would probably need one other person to help you. Books too can be very helpful, or if the restriction is in seeing, perhaps tapes and records. Music is a great source of inner experience also.

People who surround the old person or the handicapped person — doctors, nurses, well-meaning friends — all try to focus the patient on the outside world. They're upset if the patient isn't interested in the news or the family. Many older people draw inward, and maybe, from what you are saying, they need to do this kind of interior work.

I want to emphasize that there is a difference between an inner life and drawing inward. Drawing inward can be a kind of escape from the pain one feels about being humiliated by an illness. Drawing inward is hiding, while living an inner life can be enriching and rewarding. If a person so withdraws, he or she needs relationships to draw him out of hiding. These relationships can be with friends, counselors, doctors, or other healers. When that person is drawn out, he can then get a sense of a new inner dimension of life. A caring individual can pull *him* out of hiding, but not out of *himself*. The other person involved with *him* touches the healthy and creative part. . . the part which is not restricted or sick.

What about physical pain? So far we've touched mostly on chronic disabilities. What about the person who suffers constant pain from arthritis, rheumatism, hip fractures, and other afflictions which, it seems to me, could interfere even with an inner life?

Today, most pain can be controlled by medication. Actually, when we get older, nature protects us somewhat from severe pain; our sensory organs become duller. I used to dread going to the dentist. One day recently, I tried to have my teeth drilled without any anesthetic. I felt very little pain. Subsequently, I had a tooth pulled, also without anesthetic. We have a great fear of dying with pain. Some people fear that they will strangle when they die, which just doesn't happen. In a natural death, we become unconscious first and death is not painful. It's when you're living that there is pain, usually psychic pain. We now can control most severe pain with nerve blocks, medication, or hypnosis. The problem relates to the fear of pain rather than to the actuality. If the pain is not too severe, we can learn to minimize it and live with it.

In our previous conversations, you spoke of fear as a feeling from the past projected on the future. I believe you said that we experience fear in the present as anxiety.

From my experience, it isn't possible to be afraid in the present. We are afraid that something is going to happen, and fear enters and compounds the problem of pain. Expectant mothers, who are taught not to fear pain, experience none at childbirth. One of the great fears about pain is that it will never go away. We fear that perhaps something is seriously wrong. Actually, when pain is too intense, nature puts us into a state of shock, and we don't feel anything.

When I was working with nursing home patients, I often heard people cry for the nurse and say that they were in enormous pain. When the nurse came, there didn't seem to be anything drastically wrong. It seems that the cry was for help. Could it be that pain can sometimes be a call for help?

Definitely. My friend, who is a neurophysiologist, claims that pain is an opinion and a way of communicating something to another person. For example, suppose a woman suddenly contracts a headache when she and her husband have an engagement. She's communicating that something else is wrong. Perhaps she is secretly angry with her husband and takes this way of communicating her anger. In such a case, we have to learn to read what the person is trying to say with his pain.

And sometimes the person is saying "Help!"

Yes. Help me or talk to me or communicate with me. We have to learn to become more sensitive to the psychological message which the pain expresses.

It also seems that pain legitimizes asking for help. When we are well, no one pays much attention, but pain certainly is an attention-getter and sometimes gets us love and caring when we need it and can't ask for it.

But pain is also a lifesaver. It often warns us of serious trouble. If we weren't able to feel pain, we'd burn to death or lose vital organs. People who have leprosy, for instance, haven't got the ability to feel pain and therefore lose limbs and organs. So pain has a positive value. We need pain as a survival mechanism.

Hatred is life unlived.

Erich Fromm

Anger and Complaining

Anger is one of the most difficult emotions for us to deal with. We find anger offensive in others and we're afraid of our own anger. Many people have stereotypes of the older person as an angry complainer. Do you see this as true?

A lot of anger is perfectly reasonable. A person, whether older or not, needs to be angry at injustice. By the time people are 70 or 80, they have experienced plenty of injustices in life.

Yes. And when a person has experienced so many losses, lives alone, and is poor and in ill health, it would be inappropriate to be full of the joy of living. Anger must be a part of the picture. But must this anger be directed against the person's caretakers, friends, and family, or is there some other outlet?

Anger is often a cover-up for hurt and humiliation. Pride is involved and the feeling that the person has been the victim of unfair treatment. Martin Buber once wrote to Gandhi and said, "I'll fight injustice if I have to, but I'll fight lovingly."

Is it possible to fight lovingly?

Since we live in a society which seems to be built more on hate than on love, it is difficult, but it is possible.

As I think about it, I can recall clearly when an older person fought lovingly, but firmly, and won. She was an 83 year old hospitalized woman and she was very angry that the coffee had been removed from her floor to save money and would only be served at mealtimes. She organized her floor in writing petitions, wrote letters to the hospital staff, and finally to the head administrator. The coffee was returned and the lady was quite triumphant with her newly gained power.

She took effective action, which kept her from complaining. Complainers are people who won't or can't take action. Their anger is ineffectively expressed by chronic complaining.

I once worked with a group of very old nursing home patients. They were very angry with many things which were wrong at the home; the food was poor, the staff was inexperienced and uncaring, the administrator was unavailable, the nurses were insensitive. At first I was delighted to hear them express their justifiable anger, but soon meeting after meeting became a complaining outlet with one person outdoing the next with weekly horrendous tales.

Did they listen to each other or were they just eager to get their own complaints out?

That's a good question. In the beginning, no one listened to anyone else. It took a few months until a genuine caring for others returned.

It seems that the patients had temporarily lost their ability to care. They not only felt helpless to take action or responsibility for themselves, but they also felt temporarily non-caring.

Why do you say "temporarily"?

You just told me that after a few months, caring about other members in the group returned. Your being there and caring made the difference. They needed some help to begin to care again. The interaction of the human relationship releases the tension which the anger causes. If I can say, "What you said made me angry," communication is possible. Sometimes the other person becomes defensive and can't hear the reason for the anger. This person needs to defend his own hurt.

So you're saying that anger which is released either in conversation or in action will dissipate, while anger which is passive and unexpressed can lead to complaining.

Yes. Complaining is inaction. It's easier to complain than to fight. Erich Fromm stresses that we often choose to flee rather than to fight. In the case you just mentioned, the individuals took flight in complaining rather than fighting injustice. I recognize in myself a tendency to run rather than to fight.

Me too. I admire people like Maggie Kuhn of the Grey Panthers. She's in her seventies and fights for senior power. She doesn't seem to fear rejection, ridicule, or failure in her battle to gain equal rights for older people; she's releasing her anger in action. But I'm guilty of complaining. I gripe about many things in my life and environment which I don't act upon.

Let me tell you a Zen story. A man went to a Zen teacher for enlightenment. They worked for weeks and the teacher took him as far as he could, but the man was not enlightened. The teacher told him to see an old woman in the neighborhood. He sat with her patiently every day but she wasn't teaching him anything, and he wasn't gaining enlightenment. Finally, one day he said in despair, "You aren't teaching me anything! What do you have to say about that?" And she replied, "I have no complaints." And he was enlightened.

A face is a poor guarantee; nevertheless,
it deserves some consideration. And had
I the scourging of sinners, I should
deal hardest with those who belie
and betray the promises that nature
has planted on their brows.

Montaigne

Appearance

One of the great worries and even fears about growing old is the fear of being rejected because of how we look. Wrinkles, sags, grey and thinning hair, baldness, paunches... all are signs of growing older, and they are synonymous with looking unappealing. I know that we have an especially youth-oriented society which values good and young looks above all else, but I think every society has had its dreams and fantasies of staying young in old age. How do you feel about that?

I don't think that people worry so much as to how they will look when they get older. Young people, as well as middle-aged people, worry a lot about how they look now. There is certainly a fear about growing older, but concern with appearance is rooted in the present. I believe that this concern and preoccupation about looks revolves more around the issue of sexual attractiveness and of making a good professional image.

In that case, someone who is retired, who doesn't want to impress a sexual partner, should be in good shape, regardless of how he or she might look.

Yes. If these two areas are no longer of concern, then looks have no real bearing on how you feel about life. It's really an idea in your head. Many people look in the mirror a great deal; this is true of both men and women. I've known a lot of men who especially like to look in the mirror. Interestingly enough, the mirror really doesn't tell you how you look.

Really? I'm glad to hear that! Lately I haven't enjoyed mirrors so much myself.

The mirror doesn't tell you how you look because when you are looking into it, you may not be feeling very well; you are not animated, smiling, frowning, or alive-looking. You're merely looking into the mirror, perhaps looking for something. I know exactly how I look by the way I feel. I seldom look at mirrors, though I used to when I was younger. I used to be so worried because my nose wasn't in the right place.

So was I. When I was younger it was fashionable to have an upturned nose. It wasn't until Barbra Streisand made the Roman nose respectable that I felt quite comfortable about mine.

I used to think that my nose had something to do with my insecurity with women. Of course, it didn't. I really had a lot of anxiety about myself and the women picked it up. I had no confidence about living.

So you're saying perhaps that if an old person has confidence in life, she will look good to others?

That's what I'm saying. I've known old people, including older women, who were very attractive to younger partners. I had a woman of 73 come to me with the problem that younger men were interested in her and wanted to marry her. She kept turning them down. She didn't want to be that involved, and she didn't know how to deal with them. I think she felt confident about herself; she had a confidence about living which was attractive.

Is there an inner look and an outer look? Is it that some people, regardless of age, manage to look beautiful although the magazine articles and beauty schools would probably turn them totally around?

Of course. And the inner look shines through the outer look. There are many classically beautiful people with perfect features and no wrinkles who look dull and sad. On the other hand, Mrs. Roosevelt was beautiful to me, although her outward features were certainly not prepossessing. True beauty, as is said, always comes from the inside out.

I have a feeling that many people who are concerned about their looks feel that unless they look younger than they really are, they will not be admired. "My, you're looking young," seems to be the greatest compliment, whereas no one says, "My, you're feeling good!"

Actually, when you say that someone's looking young, you mean that the person looks good to you, and he looks good because you are relating to that person from within. I feel that a person who is relating to me is relating to my inner person, not my outer looks. If my eyes sparkle like those of a young man, it's because I am excited by the relationship, not because I look young. I've heard it said that you create your own face, and I feel that it's true. You're born with a certain face, and it changes all your life, but how you look as you get older is your own creation. It's created by the way you live. My face, although older, is much more relaxed than when I was younger. I was more boxed in when I was younger, and my face showed fear.

You're not just talking about the aging process in your face, but that your entire look has changed.

My entire look has changed with the way I feel. I don't ask myself the question, "How do I look?" If you ask yourself that, then the answer is likely to be "Not so good," because you're usually not satisfied with your appearance. If you are feeling good, you'll look good and you won't need to be concerned with it.

So perhaps it is all in our heads, an image again, of how we think we are supposed to look to others in order to be acceptable, even in old age. I'm reminded of a charming woman of 80 who told me she had gone to buy a lipstick and asked for a certain color. The salesgirl was out of that color and presented her with a different one, saying disdainfully, "What difference does it make?" This kind of callous attitude toward older persons often depresses them and makes them feel inferior.

It's too bad that an ignorant and insensitive salesgirl could so shatter an older person. Again, if this 80-year-old lady were feeling good about life, she would need neither the lipstick nor the affirmation of the salesgirl, but perhaps that day she needed both.

I'm still concerned with my looks, not all the time, of course, but I do have an image of myself; I like my hair a certain length and color and I sometimes wear lipstick and sometimes not, according to the way I want to look. I like my body slim and feel bad when I gain weight, and I like a certain look in clothes. I feel better when I look the way I want to look. That look isn't necessarily young, but it's attractive on my terms. I feel good when I look good. That seems to be the reverse of what you were saying. I guess I haven't arrived at a state of freedom from vanity.

You always look good to me, but that is an inner beauty I see, which has nothing to do with lipsticks or the clothes you wear. I'm reminded of an actress, a real glamour-girl in her youth. I saw her in an interview recently and she was probably in her early fifties. She was completely transformed from the woman I remembered, to a beautiful, mature person. She had grown; her looks had changed, and she was beautiful in a different way. As a young woman she'd been pretty, but now she had real beauty.

Then age isn't a factor in beauty, but if you think it is, it becomes important.

If you give so much emphasis in your life to how you look, rather than how you get along in life, you're going to undermine your own confidence in your inner self.

Would you say that goes for clothing too?

Yes. I remember talking to D.T. Suzuki, who was the first Japanese Zen teacher to bring Zen to the Western world. He said we spend too much time on our clothes. I was in a conference with him for ten days, together with a group of 40 psychiatrists and psychologists, and Suzuki wore the same suit every day. I was aware of it, but it made no difference. We want to look nice of course, and we can express our personality in clothing, but the over-emphasis interferes with living life. I'm not saying that we shouldn't dress well, but it depends on how much energy goes into the effort.

Perhaps people fear age because their outward appearance changes so much that their image of themselves is threatened.

It seems that you are saying that the inner self can change and grow and become our outer self.

When a person begins to worry inordinately about her looks, it means she has temporarily lost touch with how to live. Things are changing in her life, and she doesn't know how to deal with these changes. Teenagers often dwell on their appearance because they haven't yet acquired the inner skills to cope with the rapid changes in their lives. In middle-age, people begin to have problems because they have lost touch with a part of their lives. Perhaps they are changing, or their spouses have left, or they're switching careers; they can't deal with these new ways of living. They blame it on their looks. So you have to ask yourself, "What is the matter with the way I am living?" and not, "What is the matter with the way I look?"

Come, Sleep; O Sleep! the certain knot of peace,
The baiting-place of wit, the balm of woe,
The poor man's wealth, the prisoner's release,
The indifferent judge between the high and low.

Philip Sidney

Habits and Health

One of the cliches of aging, as well as living, is that we are creatures of habit. While this may be so, it seems that our habits can often affect us adversely. Eating, sleeping, smoking, drinking, exercising. . . all these habits seem to be up for discussion in the media today. What do you feel about some of our habits which affect our health and well-being?

Let's discuss eating, for instance. Dieting is certainly a preoccupation in American society. It's generally known today in medical circles that a low-salt, low-sugar, low-fat diet is good for the body. For the older person, a low-protein, high-carbohydrate diet is advantageous, because the older person is usually less active.

Would you say, then, that older people should watch their food intake if they wish to be healthier and more active?

I've found that it's not possible to stay on a diet because of our craving for love foods.

Love foods? What are they?

Love foods are the foods you were brought up on. I was raised on chicken soup, eggs, butter, and cheeses, all of which are a part of my Jewish culture. For other people, love foods are rice, beans, pasta, corn, candy, or whatever foods were frequently served by the mother.

These foods are associated with love because they are our earliest associations with mother?

Not only with mother, but these foods are related to companionship, family togetherness, and the renewal of love.

So, such foods are difficult for us to give up, because of the unconscious association with good feelings, and destroy our wish to diet and restrict calories.

You've heard of the law of inertia. It is a physical law, but it also relates to human activities. Our habits continue until something new enters, until another force pulls us out.

How do you see this happening? If we continue to eat something which is obviously not good for us because of the association that food has had in our life, can we break that habit?

If you put a person on a diet and he breaks the diet, that person feels guilty. The guilt creates anxiety and the anxiety causes the person to eat compulsively. Will power alone can't help someone to stay on a diet. I suggest drifting into a diet whenever possible. Sometimes this takes one or two years. Try the diet two days a week and eat accustomed love foods the rest of the time. This method will make the transition easier. We need to eat without guilt feelings. This is most important.

So, if we permit ourselves some of the love foods, it will eventually be easier to accept a diet low in sugar, salt, fat, or anything else. Perhaps we would feel virtuous about the new regime, even proud, and we wouldn't be tempted to cheat. Cheating would be legal.

Exactly. I stay on my diet only 75 percent of the time, and I don't feel guilty if I go off it.

What do you eat when you go off your diet?

Chicken soup with matzo balls, of course.

I should have known! What worries me about "drifting" into a diet over a period of a year or two, is that most people want to see immediate results. They want to be thinner or healthier and more fit right now.

Most dieters who want immediate results might indeed get them, but their newfound slimness or health doesn't last because they eventually go back to their love foods and regain weight and troublesome symptoms. In my own case, when I began my diet of 75 percent low salt, sugar, and fat, my blood chemistry showed 200 cholesterol, 150 triglyceride, and 20 blood urea nitrogen. All of these figures are in the upper range of normal for a man my age, but in my opinion this is average, not normal. Unfortunately, the average figures are too high for optimum health. After a year and a half on the diet, my cholesterol had dropped to 170, the triglyceride to 70, and the BUN to 15. My blood pressure, which had been high, returned to normal. My diet had affected my chemistry, kidney function, and blood pressure.

And you're still eating chicken soup and matzo balls.

Yes, sometimes. We don't need to be overly punitive in changing our habits. We change gradually, and usually we need the help of others. It is well known that habit abusers like alcoholics, heavy smokers, overeaters, and drug users need others to help them overcome their habit. What is needed is a new spiritual breakthrough, not a dogmatic approach through willpower alone. Sometimes suggestions from well-meaning friends or therapists are obstacles rather than incentives to change.

Are you referring to organizations like Alcoholics Anonymous, Synanon, Weight Watchers, and other group-supported and spiritually-oriented approaches to addiction?

Those organizations have all proven to be effective because individuals gain support from others who themselves had been afflicted. Actually, the ordinary dieter needs some support from other dieters who understand the difficulty in changing the habit. She will need their support until she becomes autonomous. Alcholics and recovered alcoholics actually call their new members "babies." They need to be taken care of and nurtured and are always under an older member's supervision.

How about exercise? Do we need others to activate us, or can we take care of our need for exercise alone?

Exercise is another "guilt provoker." Exercise for older people is beneficial because it serves the purpose of accelerating the heart, unless the person has severe heart disease. Of course, some enjoy various sports they have engaged in all their lives, and they may continue to enjoy them as they get older, though at a more modest pace. For the sedentary person, though, walking is a fine way to exercise and increase the heartbeat. In order to tolerate this increase, I learned to breathe deeply before taking exercise, to prevent shortness of breath.

I do notice that exercise is more enjoyable when done communally. Of course, there are solitary walkers and joggers, but many people enjoy the walk more if they have a companion. Also, there are many exercise classes for those of us who prefer not to do calisthenics alone on the floor. It does seem that a support group gets many of us exercised who would ordinarily do nothing. A gym seems like a friendlier place than a mat on the bedroom floor in front of a television screen.

We do need the support of others when we feel guilty about neglecting our physical and mental health. More and more stresses get to us when we are guilt ridden and anxious.

Perhaps I should have mentioned stress as another of life's habits. It certainly seems to plague most of us in this society with dogged regularity.

Certainly stress is a great factor in all of our health problems. I once questioned a man who was a hundred years old about his longevity. He said that he never remained in a relationship which was stressful, regardless of whether it was a work situation or a personal tie. Hans Selye, the Nobel Prize winner who studied stress, concluded that work which may be stressful is not harmful if it is welcome work and not distressful. It is prolonged unwelcomed stress that is harmful.

Is it possible to avoid stress, as the 100 year old man did?

It is probably not possible to avoid stress altogether, but it helps if we are aware of stressful situations. Sometimes, sustained stress is put on a person by a boss, a spouse, a child, a parent, or a friend. Sometimes unavoidable situations force a person to stay in a stressful relationship. It helps to realize that these situations are not of the person's own choosing or making but are enhanced by his environment. It helps to remove the guilt that person feels about the relationship.

Perhaps removing the offending relationship might set up new stresses resulting from unfamiliar surroundings, loneliness, and, as you indicated, guilt from not being able to handle the situation.

When we get into a stressful relationship or situation, we feel our body's reaction. We tighten up, have more problems with digestion, circulation, and rheumatism. Our health is definitely affected. It seems that when it comes to stress we have no sense of priorities where our own health is concerned. We make security, pride, status, and outward appearances our priorities. Actually, we would be much more useful to our family and friends if we were healthier. You mention removing the offending relationship from your life, as the hundred year old man did. It's true that a new job, a new marriage, new friends, and a new environment might set up new stresses. It is sustained stress, however, which is so harmful. We all live with temporary stress. If a man works at a job eight hours a day for thirty years and he hates every day of it, he has put himself in a sustained-stress position. If he retires and can't get along with his wife, the additional stress might kill him. It might have been better to have gotten out of the job sooner, even with a pay cut, which might have been beneficial to the marriage as well.

We often feel stuck in a job or a relationship, and the way out seems insurmountable. The stress becomes so familiar that it feels strange to be without it.

That is when many chronic illnesses begin, when constant stress is stored in the body. Today, doctors realize that stress is at the root of many medical problems. We are beginning to borrow from the Eastern philosophies and engage in meditation, yoga, imagery, acupuncture, and biofeedback, in an effort to reduce stress in our lives. These new ways of viewing the relationship between mind and body may help us one day to conquer stress as a forerunner to illness.

We mentioned sleep before as a habit which sometimes gives us trouble. It's odd that eating and sleeping should give us any trouble at all; those habits we share with all humanity as well as the animal kingdom. They seem so natural, yet we make a big thing of them. We set up more stress if we don't sleep, feel guilty if we take drugs, and tired if sleep doesn't come.

Sleep is indeed essential for refreshment, but how much sleep an individual needs is a debatable point. I have known people who lie awake at night worrying that they won't get enough sleep. Popular opinion says that one needs eight hours of sleep. I don't believe that most people need that much, especially as one gets older. As I aged, six hours or less seemed quite enough. Recently, studies have been made with depressed patients which indicate that deprivation of sleep improved their moods considerably.

I've had many clients who steadily complained about how tired they were because they didn't sleep at all. They dragged themselves around all day, remembering how they tossed and turned, read, or walked about the house. One man in his seventies told me that unless he practiced the same ritual at bedtime every night, he couldn't get to sleep. The ritual consisted of taking some mild medication from his wife (he would never ask what kind, as it differed nightly), drinking warm milk, putting a hot water bottle on his feet, and playing classical music softly on the stereo. If any of those tasks were missed, he couldn't sleep. I told him to go right ahead with them if he could sleep that way, but he said the system prevented him from going on vacation, since he could only sleep in his own bed, and he wanted to be free of dependency on the ritual.

Perhaps you could have checked with this man to see if he really did not sleep at all without the ritual. Many people complain about not sleeping, but they doze, which really has the same effect as sleep. Some persons who do sleep are not fully asleep and are aware while sleeping. Many really get enough sleep but measure by the clock rather by their body's need. If they went to bed at ten and are awake at four, they are upset and anxious. They may have had enough sleep by their inner clock, but the clock on the shelf says that they've slept only six hours, and therefore they must still be tired.

Do people sleep out of boredom as well as tiredness? I see so many people who fall asleep at movies, or in front of the T.V., or even at parties. Are these people really so tired, or are they perhaps shutting off and closing down?

Of course, boredom and escape are factors, especially in the case of older people. Young people tend to be more sleep-deprived and really need to sleep. Often the older person is more sedentary, tends to go to bed early as he doesn't know what to do with himself. This pattern may result in not sleeping, or in waking very early. Often, when people wake at three and four in the morning, loneliness and anxiety set in; fears come to the foreground. It is dark and quiet at that hour. If the person could go to bed later and wake up later when it is daylight, he may not experience so much anxiety.

What you're saying seems to be that people who are troubled about sleep should go to bed later, not be upset if they get no more than six hours of sleep, be satisfied with dozing if sleep doesn't come, and lead an active enough life so that they will be tired at night.

That sums it up pretty well. Actually, Hammond Researchers, the organization responsible for discovering cancer's correlation to smoking, showed that people who sleep nine or more hours a night are more apt to have coronary attacks and circulatory problems than those who sleep seven hours.

Children need lots of sleep, and we need less as we get older. Do you recommend less sleep, even for those people who have trouble sleeping? And how does one switch to fewer hours if one is used to getting, say, nine hours of sleep a night?

I believe that it is healthier for the older person to get about six hours of sleep. To accomplish this, a person must deliberately decrease the amount of sleep by half an hour every two weeks until they get to six hours a night. This, I feel, increases the tolerance for living.

That would mean it should take 12 weeks for a person who sleeps nine hours to get down to six a night. I guess that one of your strong habits is patience.

Well, you can't make these changes all at once. Lifetime habits are slow to change, and we must give ourselves plenty of time and assistance. It helps to involve other people in all of our changes of habit.

Involving other people seems to be a recurrent theme in our dialogue. We need others. We need a community. It's difficult to instigate changes alone and sometimes impossible. You made a statement just now about increasing tolerance for living. What did you mean by that?

I meant that when a person sleeps less, they develop more zest for life; there certainly is more time for living, but more than that, a new tolerance is built up for the stressful parts of life. If people go to sleep to avoid stressful situations, they show that they have very little tolerance for living. This tolerance is gradually built up by being awake longer and simply coping with life.

Life has no boundaries.

Dr. Ben

On Death and Dying

I wonder if old age would be feared less by the young were it not for the fact that it is the final stage of life. All other transitions — childhood to adolescence, adolescence to adulthood, youth to middle age — carry many changes, but none so drastic as that from old age to death. Old age does signify to us that we are all mortal.

That is certainly true. Old age is associated with the fear of death; the beginning of the end. It is also the fear of impairment and disability.

Would you say that our basic fear is really of dying and not necessarily of getting old?

Yes, our fears are of dying. It is an instinctive fear which we all share. A person really cannot conceive of her death consciously. If she is constantly worried about dying; however, she has a neurotic problem.

Do you mean that the instinctive fear of dying is unconscious, but if we fear death consciously we have a neurosis?

Yes. Let me illustrate. Very young children do not fear death unless instructed to do so. One of my daughters once found a worm that was broken in half; it moved for a while, but then stopped. We buried it, but that night she told me that the worm really was not dead. "How do you know?" I asked her. She replied, "Because I can see it crawling around." I knew in that moment that she had resurrected it, and that she was not afraid.

*And what about a neurotic fear of death? Have you got a
story for that aspect too?*

Yes. A former patient of mine had been afraid of dying
since he was nine years old. It affected every phase of his life,
and kept him from entering into any new phases or activities.
He seemed paralyzed by the fear of death. Believe it or not, he
lived to be 84 years old. When he was 80, he became quite
senile, and when he died, he didn't even know he was dying. He
recognized no one and was totally unconcerned with death.
All of those years, the man was very resistant to changes in his
life, which was really due to a fear of dying.

*You mean that this man died a little every time he had to
make a change in his life? That change was so terrible for him
that he could not conceive of this final, great change?*

Yes. Dying to the old and beginning the new can be very
frightening; especially if changes are forced upon us, changes
which we would rather not make. Illness forces us into new
ways of living, friends or relatives die, children leave, we go
through a divorce. We resist these changes and they are experienced as a fear of dying. There is another implication as well;
to keep the status quo. If we have learned to live in the
present, there is no room in our minds for dying. We fear
dying because we have not consciously fully lived, and life
seems incomplete. If one is fully alive and living every moment,
what is there to miss by dying? We will have done it all.

*My feeling is that although I do live fully, I still may miss
a lot by dying.*

Well, if you have that feeling, perhaps there are areas of
living which are blocked off in the present, without your being
aware of them. If your life is meaningful day by day, you aren't

missing anything. You cannot have more than life. There isn't any more. If you are truly alive, you have touched the eternal life source, and there just isn't any more than this.

I guess I'm just greedy; I want more of a good thing. It's kind of like saying, "Oh, can't the party last a little longer?" or the child in me saying, "Can't I stay up a little bit later so I won't miss anything?"

Yes, it's the child in you that wants life to last longer. It's natural for a child to want the party to go on and on. But you're an adult now, and it is possible to learn to understand "time." If you are living in the eternal "Now," there is no clocked time. If you measure living by the clock, you're using an arbitrary standard, an outer standard, not an inner one. John Lilly, a well-known scientist and author, constructed a tank of water which was relatively soundproof and close to body temperature. I floated in this tank for approximately an hour and a half. I was floating on about ten or twelve inches of salt water, which makes one very buoyant. A woman came out to tell me that I had been floating for an hour and a half and it was time to leave. I had no conception of time whatsoever and thought it had been no more than twenty minutes. I had lost the outward sense of time. The point is, if you function on your inner clock, you lose the sense of outer time. If you're worried about not lasting longer, however, you are looking at the outer clock.

It seems that this is an important point in our ability to age creatively, or joyously, as you put it. If we could lose concern with the outer clock, then aging would not have the unhealthy significance of "time passing us by."

It is important to understand this inner-outer clock theory in terms of aging. When you are young, there is plenty of time; children naturally live in the present with their inner clock.

They aren't hungry on our schedule of outer time; they "lose" themselves in play and resent being brought back to the outer clock. It's too bad that we lose this ability to pay attention to the inner clock which we all have. The outer clock is necessary for keeping appointments, going to work and going to a movie... but your inner life is not judged by that kind of time. At this point in my life, I am not concerned with time, but I was when I was younger.

This view of inner and outer time came out of our discussion about the fear of death. How do you personally feel about dying? Are you afraid to die at this point in your life?

I am not afraid of dying, but I do fear being incapacitated, especially by a stroke. If I couldn't talk, that would be much worse than dying. After all, talking is my profession; I've spent my life talking. Anything else I could tolerate, as long as I could talk. Let me add, though, that this fear indicates to me that I still haven't achieved a perfect trust in life. If I had that, I wouldn't think about having a stroke unless it happened... I'd be too busy just living.

Well, that makes me feel good. You are still growing and learning.